The Little Makana

by Helen M. Dano
Illustrated by Wren

Bess Press
P. O. Box 22388
Honolulu, Hawaii 96823

For my Makana, Mom, and Makana's
Auntie Carol, who helped name him

H. M. D.

For my own *makana*, Elijah Gabriel

W.

Cover design: Paula Newcomb

"*Pūpū Hinuhinu*" © Nona Beamer
"Hawaiian Lullaby" © Peter Moon and Hector Venegas
"Makana's Lullaby" © Helen M. Dano

Library of Congress Catalog Number: 94-77956

There is a wondrous word in the Hawaiian
language for "gift" and that is *makana*.

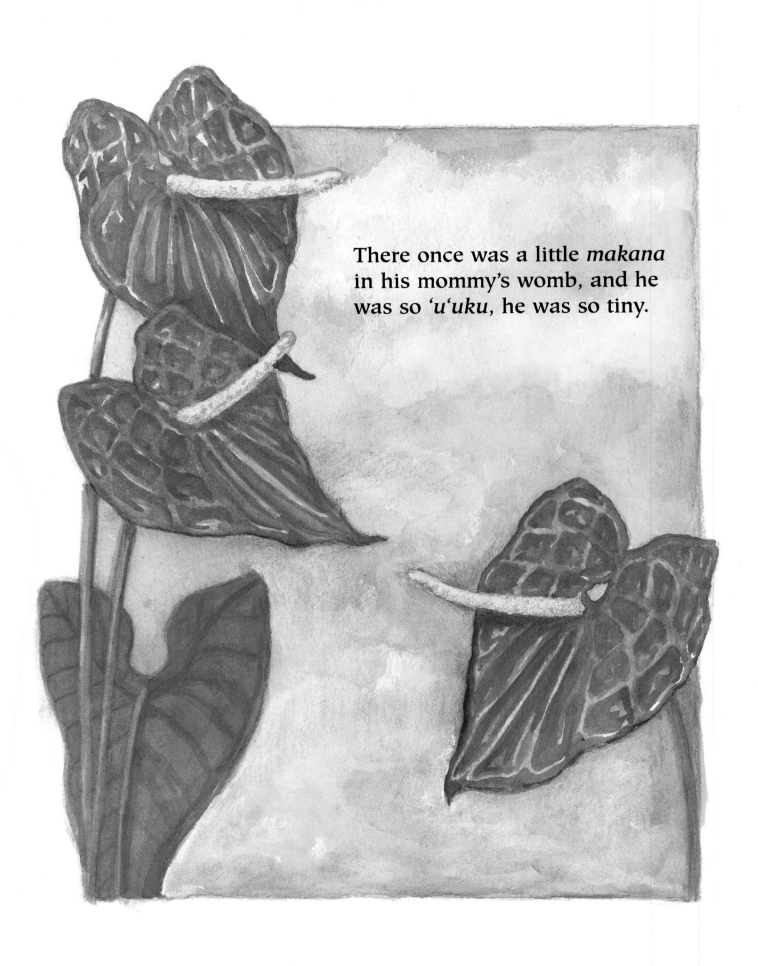

There once was a little *makana* in his mommy's womb, and he was so *'u'uku*, he was so tiny.

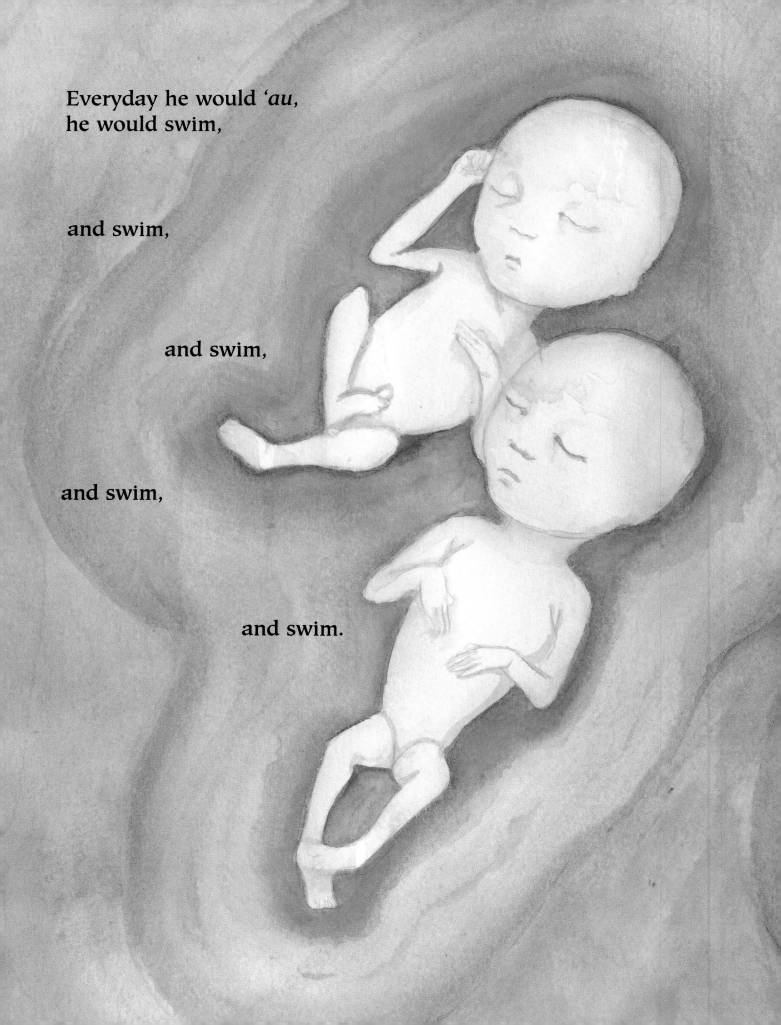

Everyday he would '*au*,
he would swim,

and swim,

and swim,

and swim,

and swim.

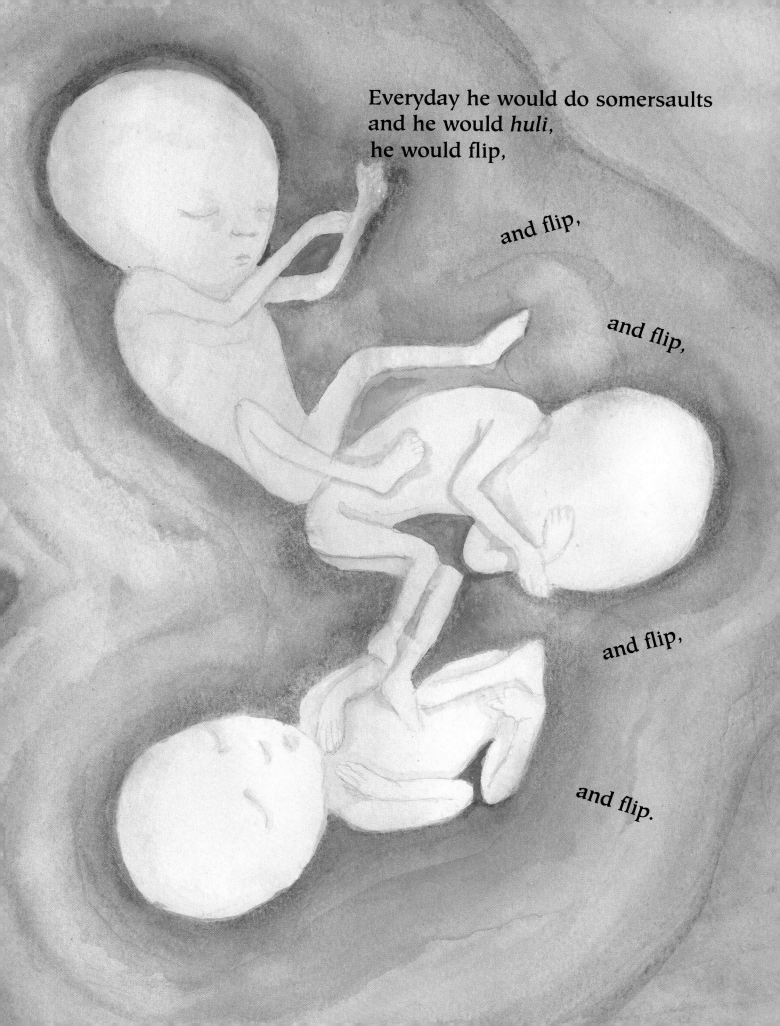

Everyday he would do somersaults
and he would *huli*,
he would flip,

and flip,

and flip,

and flip,

and flip.

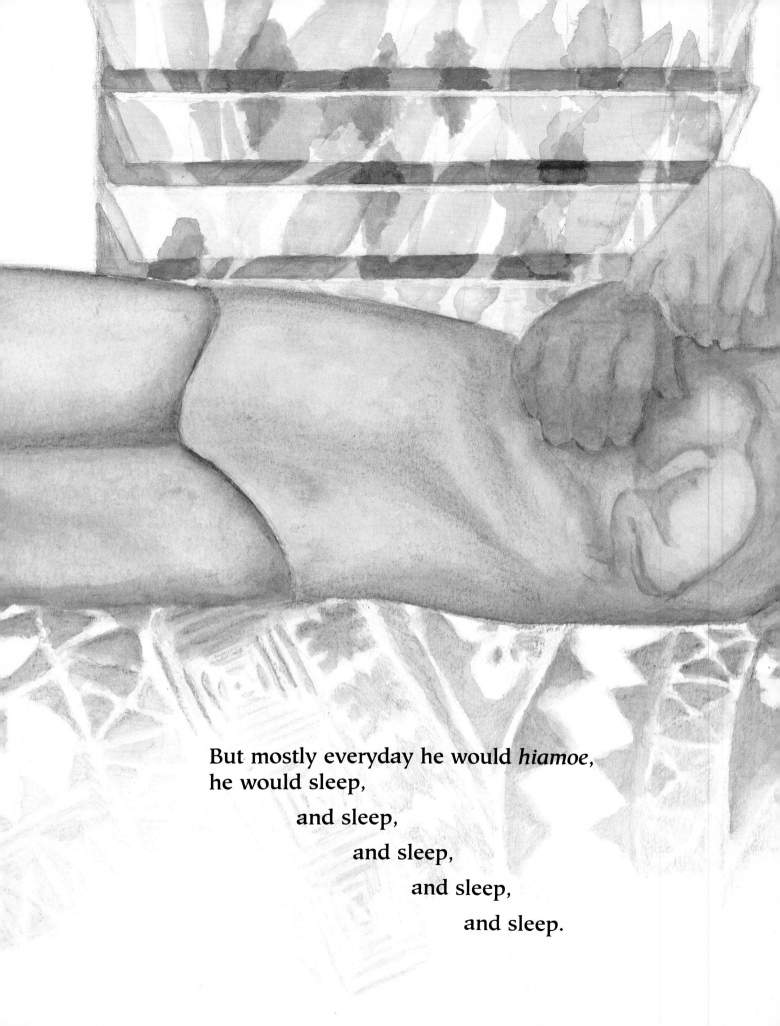

But mostly everyday he would *hiamoe*,
he would sleep,

and sleep,

and sleep,

and sleep,

and sleep.

Now every morning he would hear his mommy say,

"*Aloha kakahiaka*,
Good morning, my *keiki*, my child.
How are you today?"

And the little *makana* in his mommy's womb
would stop what he was doing
and he would *mino'aka*,
he would smile,
because his mommy was talking to him.

He didn't know what she was saying,
but he knew,
he knew she was talking to him
and that made him so *hau'oli*, so happy,
he would smile.

She would ask him,
"What shall we *'ai*, what shall we eat for
breakfast today?"
He'd smile.

"Shall we have pineapple juice or a papaya?"
He'd smile.

"Shall we have eggs with Portuguese sausage?"
He'd smile.

"Or shall we have coconut
syrup on french toast made
with sweet bread?"
He'd smile.

"Or should we just have
a bowl of cold mango slices?"
He would do a somersault
and then he'd smile.

Throughout the day the little *makana*
would hear all kinds of noises and sounds,
like the roar of waves breaking on shore,
or water falling,
or music playing,
or people *e mele ana*, singing,
or *e kama'ilio ana*, talking,
and sometimes his mommy would talk
to these people sounds and at other times
she wouldn't.

Sometimes he would be
so frightened of these
sounds that he would *lelele,*
he would bounce,

and bounce,

and bounce,

and bounce,

and bounce.

And then he'd hear his mommy say,
"Now, now, my *keiki*. It's all right.
Hush, hush . . ."

And the little *makana* would settle
into a calm in his mommy's womb
and he would smile.

Most of the day, the little *makana* would
be very busy with his swimming and his
somersaults, but especially his sleeping.

He would sleep so much
that the next thing he knew
he would hear his mommy say,
"Good night, my *keiki. Aloha ahiahi.*
Thank you for another *lā,*
for another day."

And the little *makana*
in his mommy's womb
would s – t – r – e – t – c – h ,
and then he'd smile,
for his Mommy was talking to him.
He didn't know what she was saying,
but he knew,
he knew she was talking to him.
And that made him so happy
that he would smile.

Before she slept,
she would sing him lullabies.
First, she would sing *"Pūpū Hinuhinu."*
Next, she would sing "Hawaiian Lullaby."

Pūpū Hinuhinu

Words and music by Nona Beamer

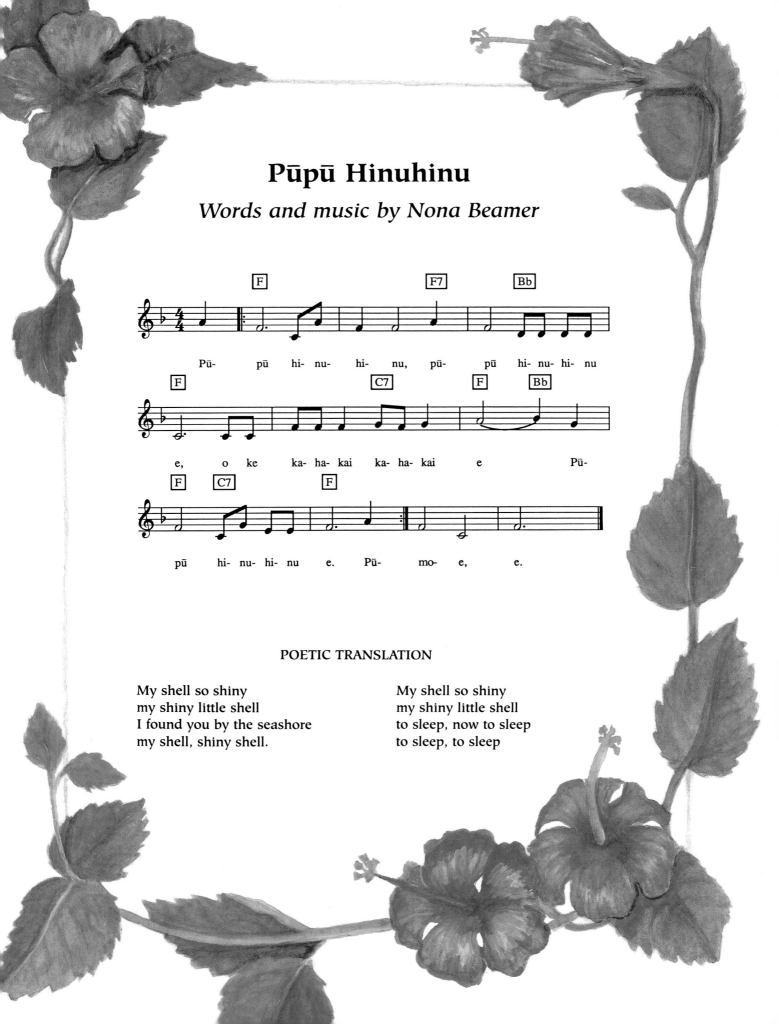

Pū- pū hi- nu- hi- nu, pū- pū hi- nu- hi- nu

e, o ke ka- ha- kai ka- ha- kai e Pū-

pū hi- nu- hi- nu e. Pū- mo- e, e.

POETIC TRANSLATION

My shell so shiny
my shiny little shell
I found you by the seashore
my shell, shiny shell.

My shell so shiny
my shiny little shell
to sleep, now to sleep
to sleep, to sleep

Hawaiian Lullaby

Lyrics by Peter Moon and Hector Venegas

Music by Peter Moon

And then she would sing a song
she made up just for her *makana*.
He knew she created it for him
because the words would often change;
sometimes the melody would change, too.

Makana's Lullaby

Words and music by Helen M. Dano

Musical notation by Ray Allen

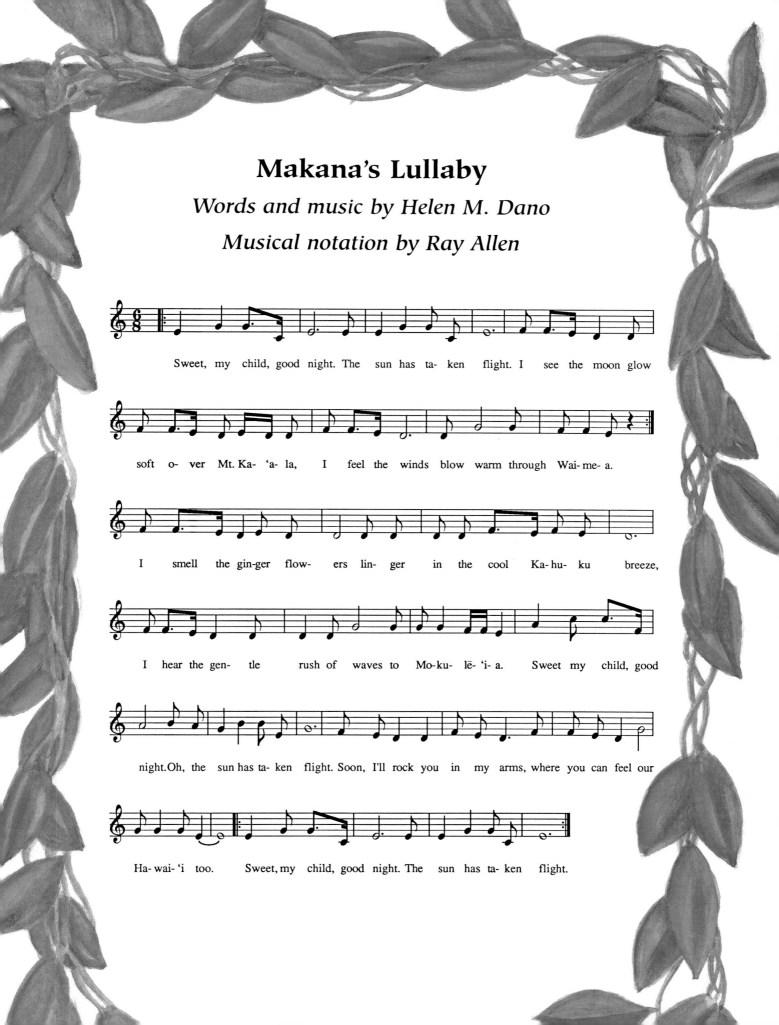

Sweet, my child, good night. The sun has ta- ken flight. I see the moon glow

soft o- ver Mt. Ka- 'a- la, I feel the winds blow warm through Wai- me- a.

I smell the gin-ger flow- ers lin- ger in the cool Ka-hu- ku breeze,

I hear the gen- tle rush of waves to Mo-ku- lē- 'i- a. Sweet my child, good

night.Oh, the sun has ta- ken flight. Soon, I'll rock you in my arms, where you can feel our

Ha- wai- 'i too. Sweet, my child, good night. The sun has ta- ken flight.

And the little *makana* would
be so sleepy again.
But just before he'd drift off,
he would hear his mommy say,
"'Night, 'night, my *keiki.*
Aloha au iā 'oe, I love you."

And the little *makana*,
as tired as he was,
would smile.

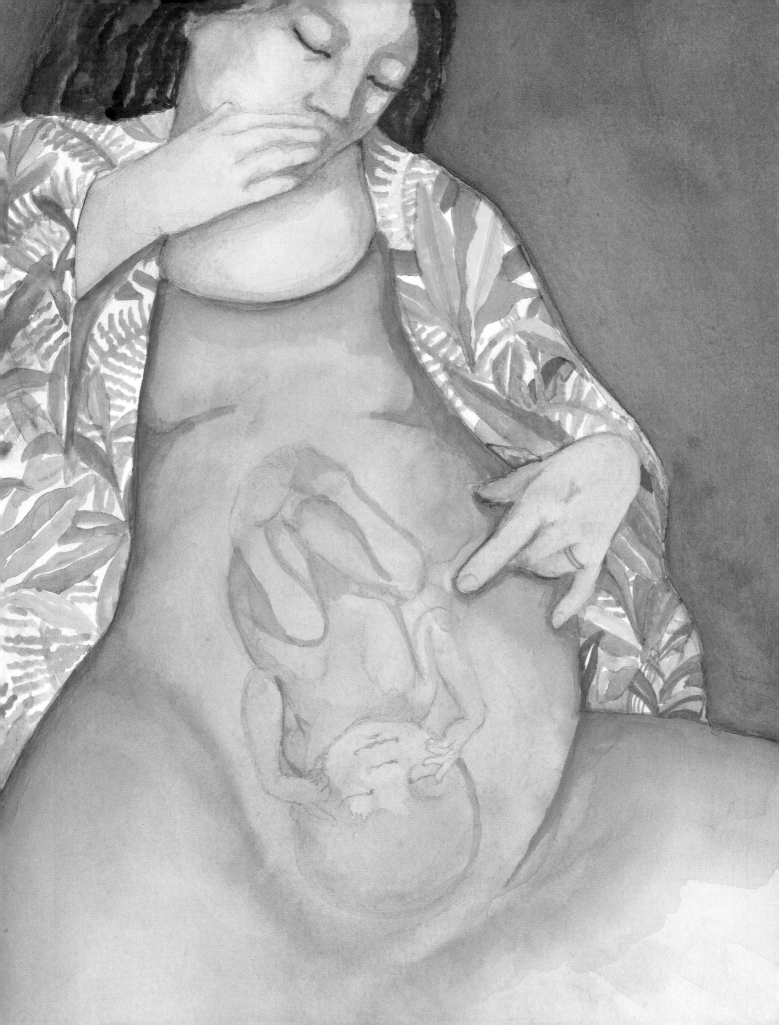

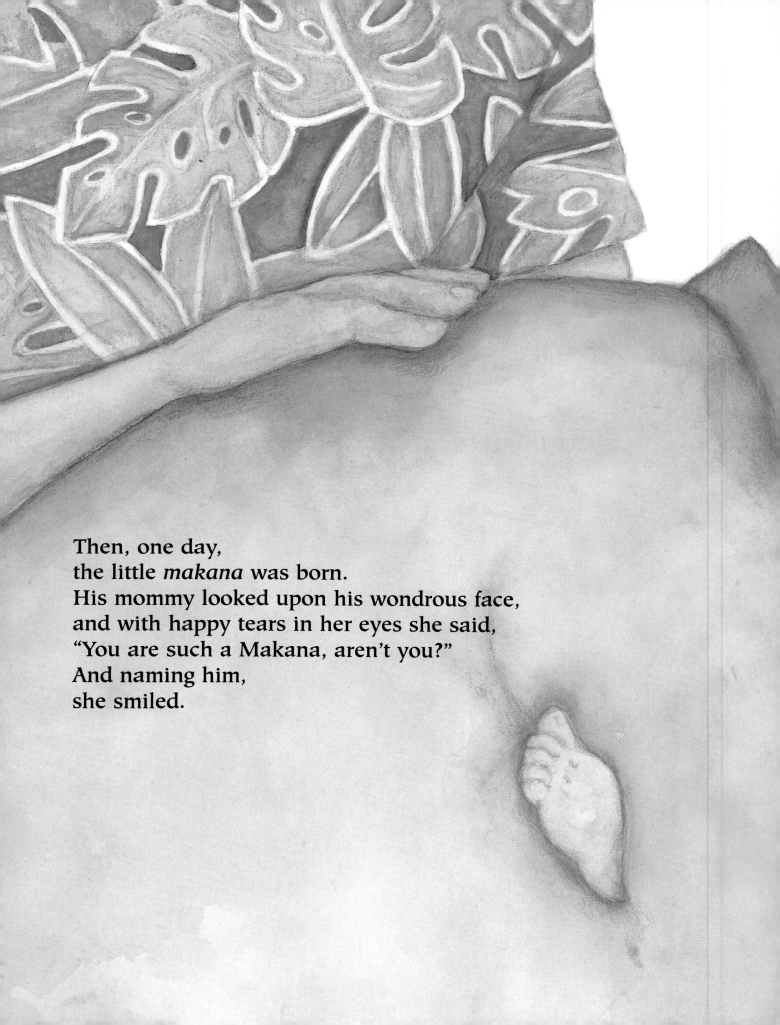

Then, one day,
the little *makana* was born.
His mommy looked upon his wondrous face,
and with happy tears in her eyes she said,
"You are such a Makana, aren't you?"
And naming him,
she smiled.

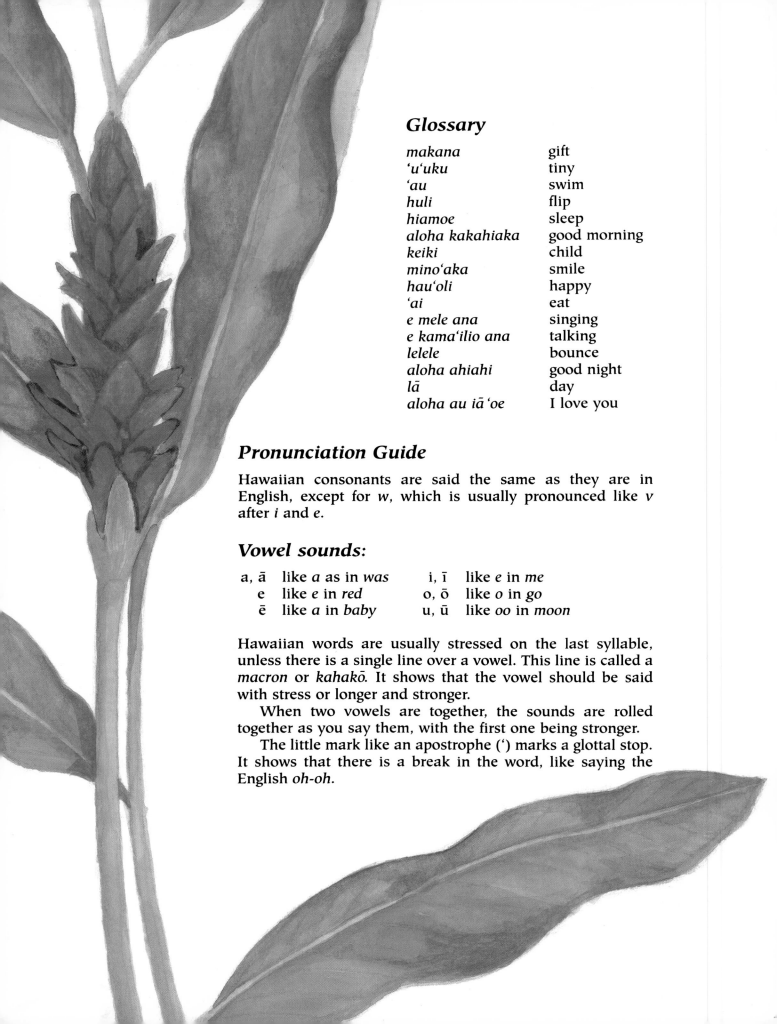

Glossary

makana	gift
'u'uku	tiny
'au	swim
huli	flip
hiamoe	sleep
aloha kakahiaka	good morning
keiki	child
mino'aka	smile
hau'oli	happy
'ai	eat
e mele ana	singing
e kama'ilio ana	talking
lelele	bounce
aloha ahiahi	good night
lā	day
aloha au iā 'oe	I love you

Pronunciation Guide

Hawaiian consonants are said the same as they are in English, except for *w*, which is usually pronounced like *v* after *i* and *e*.

Vowel sounds:

a, ā	like *a* as in *was*		i, ī	like *e* in *me*
e	like *e* in *red*		o, ō	like *o* in *go*
ē	like *a* in *baby*		u, ū	like *oo* in *moon*

Hawaiian words are usually stressed on the last syllable, unless there is a single line over a vowel. This line is called a *macron* or *kahakō*. It shows that the vowel should be said with stress or longer and stronger.

When two vowels are together, the sounds are rolled together as you say them, with the first one being stronger.

The little mark like an apostrophe (') marks a glottal stop. It shows that there is a break in the word, like saying the English *oh-oh*.